Firehouse
Coloring Book

Cathy Beylon

DOVER PUBLICATIONS, INC.
Mineola, New York

Note

The job of the firefighter is a very important one. He or she helps put out fires and rescues those in danger. Firefighters also visit schools to teach fire safety. Some fire departments have emergency medical teams. They ride in ambulances and take care of injured people. You will learn all about the men and women who work at the firehouse as you enjoy coloring the pictures in this book.

Copyright

Copyright © 2000 by Cathy Beylon
All rights reserved.

Bibliographical Note

Firehouse Coloring Book is a new work, first published by Dover Publications, Inc., in 2000.

International Standard Book Number
ISBN-13: 978-0-486-41308-2
ISBN-10: 0-486-41308-X

Manufactured in the United States by RR Donnelley
41308X08   2016
www.doverpublications.com

Fighting fires is an important job in any town or city. Your local firefighter is there to help in times of trouble.

The firehouse, or station, is where firefighting equipment is kept and the firefighters work throughout the day when not answering an alarm.

Firefighters wear heavy clothing to protect
themselves from fire.

4

Here are a rubber jacket, boots,
a helmet, and overalls.

5

Cindy wears pants, a jacket, boots, and a helmet
when she answers a call for help.

Maria is a member of the emergency medical
team that works with the firefighters.

In between calls, the firefighters keep busy. Ray is washing the fire truck until it is clean and shiny.

The firefighters cook and eat many of their meals on the job. Ray enjoys cooking for his friends.

Sparky, a dalmatian, has a great time being
the firehouse dog!

A firefighter visits schools to teach fire safety. Children learn to "Stop" what they are doing, "Drop" to the floor, and "Roll" around to keep their clothes from burning.

11

People can send a fire alarm from a call box like the one shown here. Firefighters connect a hose to a fire hydrant to get water.

There is no time to lose to rescue this woman!

The alarm sounds, and Ray grabs his helmet and jacket.

Cindy slides down the pole—the fastest way
to get to the fire truck.

The fire truck is on its way.

Cars move over to let it pass.

This firefighter has a floodlight to help him see.

Another firefighter has an ax to break down walls.

This is an aerial ladder truck.

The ladder can be raised high to rescue people.

The fire department sends an ambulance to the scene.

It will take any injured people to a nearby hospital.

The fire chief often travels in a separate car
to the scene of a fire.

Firefighters have to be strong to carry
the hose up a ladder.

The firefighters rescue the woman.

With hard work they put out the fire.

Fire trucks often ride in parades.

This truck proudly flies its banner.

The fire chief hopes that you enjoyed learning about the firehouse and firefighters.